GOD, ME and the MANGO TREE

Paula Rule

Paula Rule

Go, Me and the Mango Tree
© Paula Rule
Memoir/Mind, Body, Spirit
Some names have been changed for legal reasons.

ISBN: 978-0-6485938-9-8 Paperback

ISBN: 978-0-6486888-0-8 E-Book

ALL RIGHTS RESERVED

Contents

Soul Power	1
Glory of Love	36
Ecstasy of Spirit	67
Bradley	88
Chris	90
Paul	95
The Duty of Love	97
Three Levels of Soul Ascension	99
Suggested Reading	103
Links	105
About the Author	107

Paula Rule

Soul Power

Suffer little children to come unto Me for theirs is the kingdom of Heaven. Luke 18:16

Father always said he never wanted any of us. Mother was a sexual predator and paedophile. Bill and Jean Lowden lived for money and sex and made sure they had plenty of both.

They portrayed themselves as good Catholics and had numerous children who were immediately neglected. I never felt comfortable calling those people my parents, or mum, or dad. The older kids just referred to them as the old girl and the old boy, or the olds. Younger ones were left in the 'care' of the elder children. I still bear scars from that time.

At school I fainted from hunger because mother didn't provide food. I ate fruit from neighbour's trees and received a container of milk at school. A kind girl in my class, Rachael used to share her lunch with me.

Thanks to free university study at that time, the olds became 'professional' people and moved to an affluent suburb. Nobody knew what went on behind their closed doors. Nine of us were jammed into a three bedroom house. Cockroaches crawled amongst rubbish on filthy floors. There was rarely food for breakfast and no lunch. Jumpers or shoes weren't provided and I had to lie to the teacher, telling her I'd forgotten them or risk getting bashed if I told the truth. When I wept in despair my 'family' mocked and ridiculed me so I learned to react with anger and a sharp tongue.

I was forced to share a single, rusted and broken bed with my sister, Rita. The olds weren't big on providing blankets either so our combined body heat kept us warm. During the day I'd jump around in the sunshine for that same reason.

I always hoped the people who were supposed to be my family would love and protect themselves, and each other, but those hopes were never realized. We were all abused by sick relationships that were rooted in evil. Through God's love and protection of His purpose, I endured and continued to flourish in a living hell.

Mother's eldest children were teenagers then and she used them to procure adolescent boys for her to molest. She'd provide them with alcohol and drugs. I was seven years old, locked in her car, staring at the sickening sight of her gangbanging my brother's high school friends on the bank of a local creek.

My eldest sister, Carmel was fourteen when she met a young man named Rod. Mother encouraged her to have sex with him and they had sex all over the house.

The old girl said he could live with us. I thought he was a sleaze and hated him, especially when she would buy and prepare a big breakfast for him when we had none. I'd never seen her prepare breakfast for anyone. The old girl would send my sister out on errands and while she was gone, mother would be having sex with her boyfriend.

Within weeks of each other the old girl and my sister both became pregnant to Rod. Carmel was expelled from school because of her condition so mother got special permission for her to marry. The old boy was against it but she was set on her evil plan. Mother found a job for my sister and while she was out of the house the old girl and Rod would be having sex on the floor. Rod began beating my sister.

I told father everything. In my innocence, I thought if the evil was exposed and dealt with, it would go away. I couldn't have known mother had ripped out his balls years before I was born.

The old boy finally confronted her one evening with the truth. She was screaming, *'Who told you!'* over and over again.

I heard him say, 'It was Paula'.

The old girl came storming out of their room her face contorted with fury. Her crazed eyes fixed on me as she spat, 'You little bastard!'

Everything goes dark after that.

The old girl hated me and my brother Tony as we refused to be bought or corrupted. We knew instinctively we should have a safe and loving home so we rebelled and were bashed and starved. The others went along with the situation or pretended it wasn't happening so they were given food and money.

To get home from school and see strange people having sex on the dirty lounge room floor was disgusting and scary. I made cubby houses in the back yard out of discarded rubbish and spent most of my childhood there. My favourite place was in the mango tree. My home in its branches was peaceful, and I was safe there in the sure knowledge I was loved by God.

Every year the mango tree was pregnant with fragrant, succulent fruit that sustained me. The sun, shining in a changing kaleidoscope of light on soft green leaves, filled me with happiness. The serenity and clarity of thought I found in its shade enabled me to write poetry and short stories. It was difficult to be creative in their house. The filth and cockroaches were all too real, just like the cold and hunger, and the knowledge I was unloved and unwanted.

Eternal love was just God, me, and the mango tree.

I feared mother and tried to stay out of her way. The ugliness at her core leeched out into her appearance. She was cursed with a hardened face and a square, squat body. Her hands stank like old fish and none of us were encouraged to wash. I loved being clean so when they weren't around I'd shower at least once a day.

The old girl continued abusing alcohol and drugs and ran away when she was eight months pregnant to my sister's husband. Every day she was gone we'd hide around the house because when the old boy came home he'd strap the first kid he found. When she was sure he'd put up with the situation she came back. Mother was still seeing Rod but now the old boy knew, she said he could sleep in *my* cubby. The old girl continued to see Rod and pay him for sex.

I'd just turned eight when I was called out of class to go and see her baby. When we got to the hospital father was crying, pointing to a baby that was clearly not his, saying, 'That's not my son!' The old boy was a redhead and about half of us looked like him. He told the others they could be anyone's kid.

I was forced to look after her baby and if he was hurt in my care I was belted repeatedly. Rod's child didn't stand a chance. From his birth mother would encourage him to masturbate on her nude body. Then all through his childhood she would 'pick the worms out of his bottom' as she put it. Carmel was sent away, alone with her young son. She was sixteen. Rod committed suicide.

Mother enrolled us in Catholic school to keep up her façade of being a religious woman. She still wouldn't provide food but because of the dress code we had school shoes. The nuns that taught us were good, decent women who dedicated their lives to helping others and I finally had role models I could look up to. The saints were my heroes. I loved school; it was a breath of fresh air and a safe and caring environment.

I used to sit in the silent interior of the church in the school grounds and commune with God. Sometimes I'd take money from the poor box to buy lunch and feel terrible shame and hatred for my mother. I *knew* the Lord loved me. If my parents would not provide for basic needs then He would. If the olds had been poor I would have suffered going without food and warm clothes with dignity, but they were both professional people who lived a lie. Hypocrites who pretended to love the Lord at church, then went home to use and abuse their many children.

1977 was a good year. I was twelve then. Even though the old girl refused to buy the dress I needed, nuns provided a spare one and I was confirmed into the Catholic faith. My Godparents, whom I could not recall seeing before, came to present me with a gold chain and gold star pendant. At its heart was an aquamarine gem - my birthstone. They left straight after giving me the chain that I reverently placed around my neck. I didn't get to wear it for five minutes. Rita was jealous and ripped it from my throat. I never saw my lovely gift again.

Early one morning my sister Janet woke me from sleep to tell me she just gangbanged some guys on the footpath. She was fifteen years old. I seriously though of becoming a nun but what I wanted more than anything was a loving family.

Janet got parts in some plays and mother kept an album of photographs of the characters she played. I co-starred in a live theatre production that year and of course the olds weren't interested in seeing my performance or keeping any mementos, no school photos, nothing. In fact after I got a leading role we were pulled out of drama class. No matter what opportunities came my way they wouldn't help me; they'd do what they could to destroy any success I might achieve.

Even though great things were happening for me on the surface, the neglect and abuse was so hurtful that when the older siblings offered me cigarettes, alcohol and pot, I took it all gladly. They used marijuana to enhance their sexual experiences but to me it was a spiritual aid. I was able to focus more on the Lord's love for me and was strengthened to endure.

I think the deepest pain from childhood was that I couldn't save my brothers and sisters. They didn't thank me for caring; they actually hated me for trying to expose the truth. They mocked and made fun of me, calling me 'Saint Paula'. My effort, heartbreak and tears had been wasted on a situation not in my power to change. I focused on my own life, looking forward to relationships based on love and trust where I could fulfil my purpose as a child of God.

That year I began cleaning their house in the hope they would be inspired to do so. How could I invite friends over to that pigsty? The olds would sit on the couch picking their noses and wipe snot on the chairs. When I went into their room I opened a cupboard they kept locked. It was full of gourmet meals and bottles of vitamins. Knowing they shut themselves in there to gorge on food while their children were hungry made me angry. I confronted the old girl and told her I was going to tell people what she was doing to us. She threatened to send me to a bad girl's home where, she told me, they'd shave my head.

As mother was having sex with anyone she could we were always receiving crank calls. One was different. The old girl told us we had a sister they placed in an institution when she was a baby, before we were born. She was now twenty-four, and on her way over! When she arrived we thought she was beautiful. She only had one hand so we knew why they dumped her. When she asked why she was discarded the old girl said, 'You were just an inconvenient lump in my stomach.'

***

High school was so much fun. There were no males to fight over at an all-girls school so the girls had no need to be bitchy. Learning was a joy and I had a few friends. I was fourteen when the olds dropped me off at a youth gathering, in a borrowed outfit, to catch a boyfriend.

I met Jason; a seventeen year old. He seemed like a nice guy and it wasn't until years later I learned that virgins were his specialty. I'd only give up my virginity for love and he did seem to love me. He'd hitchhike to our house and sleep in the park so he could see me for the whole day. He was very patient and said he would wait until I was ready. After a few months he gave me a friendship ring and that caused a sensation at school as I was the first in my class to get one. Even the trendy girls wanted to hear all about my older boyfriend. I told them he gave me the ring because I kept my legs closed and if they wanted romance they should not throw their virginity away out of curiosity for sex.

I went to sleepovers at friends' houses and their beautiful homes and families left me longing for a love I'd never known in this life. I begged the old boy to get a divorce for all our sakes. He would not look me in the eye when he said, 'It's my cross to bear.'

What about the eight children they were abusing?

I worked at a health food shop in the school holidays to buy my own clothes. One item I purchased was a soft lemon coloured skirt. It was still new when the old girl told me to let Rita borrow it to wear to a riverbank piss-up. She had the same selfish, uncaring attitude as mother and I knew my beautiful skirt would be ruined. I woke up to find it discarded on the floor covered with cigarette burns and grass stains.

Before work one day I was in great pain. I told the olds but they didn't care. By that evening the pain was unbearable and they still refused to take me to hospital. Tony's girlfriend, a junkie, insisted they take me. I was admitted immediately suffering appendicitis. When I woke up from the operation my boyfriend was the only one there. He said he had a surprise for me and took off his shirt. On his arm was a tattoo of my name in a heart.

I was expected to leave home at fifteen so Jason and I moved to the Gold Coast. He got a job as a groundsman in a resort and I worked at a bikini shop. We shared a small flat at Surfers Paradise and I hoped I could finally have a life of love.

After Jason took my virginity he became cruel and would stay at the nightclub in the resort where he worked until dawn. I'd wander the streets of Surfers alone at night wondering why I wasn't getting the love I craved. Maybe it was my fault, maybe I expected too much of people. I started harming myself, cutting myself with broken glass. Jason began abusing me in earnest. He bashed and sexually assaulted me.

My parents were holidaying nearby so I went there and asked if I could stay with them. The old girl sat on the steps and cried and said if I stayed, she would leave.

There was a teenage girl living with them then, another needle user. Her name was Amy. She said she was disgusted by the olds too but wouldn't say anything as she needed the roof over her head. She advised me not to care so much.

I started going out with Greg. He and I loved each other but in their way his parents were as bad as mine. They considered their two sons to be their property and to this day their sons are drug addicts who never married.

Greg's father was often drunk and demanded I sit on his lap. When I refused he'd get angry and Greg's mother told me to sit on his knee to shut him up. I slept at Greg's place whenever I could to get away from the olds but his father was always bursting in when I was drying off after a shower. I woke up once to find his hand under my skirt.

Greg told his parents we were moving out together. His father was drunk, as usual, and went mental. He stood up, swearing, and ripped my dress off. He picked me up to throw me off their balcony when Greg jumped on his back to stop him. Next thing I knew I was standing there in shock when

Greg's mother walked over to me and said, 'Cover yourself up, you little slut!'

I was devastated. I thought other people would be better than my parents but I was learning there were a lot of bad people around. Greg and I lived together for about a year but his parents tore us apart.

I was a receptionist then and moved into a flat close to work. I loved my job and my freedom. My place was kept spotlessly clean. I had a great boss who was professional and kind, more like a dad than a boss. His name was Phil and a year later he moved interstate. Phil really was like a dad to me. He was also my confidant and mentor. Phil stayed in contact and we remain close friends.

Some nights I went to the city with a girlfriend and met Kevin at a club. He was heir to a nice estate in the wealthy western suburbs. He moved in to my flat a few months later. We tried to make a go of it but the feeling just wasn't there so I asked him to leave.

A friend of mine met someone named Bradley at the local sporting club and insisted I meet him. We went there that weekend to play in the pool competition and there was a guy who stood out from everyone else. The way he leaned over the pool table accentuated his long, lean body. His amber eyes were framed by long black lashes and his expression was serious as he sighted the ball. I'd never seen a more handsome man.

Nick had raved about this guy and I understood why. He was larger than life, so good looking it was impossible not to stare or want to know more about him. Bradley was the centre of attention and played a killer game of pool. He came across as so confident, yet down to earth, that men and women were irresistibly drawn to him.

He told us he was at loose ends because he'd recently broken up with a woman he'd been with for five years and she was the mother of his baby son. He said he was staying with a female friend for a roof over his head. There was an attraction between us and we began hanging out.

To be in Bradley's presence was an uplifting experience. I felt beautiful, alive! One day he took me to a house where he was able to see his son for a short time. Seeing him with his little boy stole my heart. He was all gentle patience and total love and I knew I wanted some of that love too but I couldn't let him know that. He might laugh at me or reject me. Besides, he apparently wasn't over what went down with his ex.

I was staying at Rita's then and Bradley arranged to visit me there even though it meant a long train journey. As soon as he arrived my sister started being nasty so Bradley and I settled into our room for the night. Emerald sheets covered a mattress on the floor, the only furniture in the room. A skylight in the ensuite provided a soft, natural light.

Without words he slowly undressed us both, his eyes never leaving mine. He laid me on the emerald sheets as his hands slid down my body. I could see his reflection in the mirrored wall behind him and his back and buttocks were totally muscled. It was awesome to feel this beautiful man making love to me. His hands were like silk all over my body and I finally knew what it was like to be made love to.

We awoke with the sunrise and my sister's children. They were crying for food so Bradley and I fed them. While I was cleaning the kitchen Bradley picked up a guitar that was there and started playing some soft, beautiful music I'd never heard before. There seemed to be a feeling of magic in the air that was shattered with the emergence of my sister and her boyfriend. They told me I had to leave. I had nowhere to go and said I would kill myself.

Bradley reluctantly said I could stay at the house he and his brothers were renting. It was obvious he didn't want me there but it was the only accommodation available.

His brothers were sniggering and making crude jokes so I understood why he wasn't keen on me being there. He told them I was just a friend who needed a place to stay and that was true. No words had been spoken between us and I was too vulnerable to be the first to speak. Bradley was different around his brothers, acting cool and macho.

Women buzzed around him like bees around a flower and he had many female friends. Maybe he made love like that to everyone? The love I felt for him kept getting stronger and I knew no matter what happened I would love him completely, forever.

It wasn't long before Bradley's ex showed up and I could see how upset he was; even though he was pretending everything was cool. Clara was a good looking, dark-skinned woman and their son was gorgeous. What was Bradley doing with me, a redhead?

I asked him what happened with her. He said she'd been unfaithful while he was away for work. Shattered by her betrayal, he would cry about what she had done and said he could never be with her again.

She seemed determined to screw with him and make life difficult. She'd show up unannounced, with no provisions and dump their son on Bradley, saying she was going north for a week or so. We were unemployed then and both of us put in to provide his baby with the basics.

The way she treated her son and Bradley showed me she was a heartless bitch that didn't deserve him. So why was he still crying about her? I felt I had to protect my own feelings and the next time he cried about her, I told him if he was so upset about her then maybe he should run back to her.

It was hard work staying with the Castle brothers. Bradley would take off, sometimes for days and I'd stay in his room to avoid cynical jokes about me being there. When he was home he'd work in the garden and piece together an old car he planned to get on the road. At night we'd go to bed fully clothed. There was no sex. One day he said he was ready to work out west again and would be away for six weeks.

During this time I was able to rent a small flat. The night before he left we shared a candlelit bath together. We could not take our eyes off each other. No words were spoken. There was no sexual contact. I lay back and enjoyed the sight of him. He was all male even with bubbles up to his chest. His expression was serious and his eyes glowed in the flickering light.

***

He sent letters saying he was longing to embrace me, that he missed me. Kevin was trying to get back with me and I allowed him to escort me to nightclubs. What was Bradley doing out west? Was he going out with dark-skinned women or getting his rocks off whenever he felt like it?

All I knew was that I wanted Bradley and would daydream about our future together. I'd only been hanging out with him for a few months and we were officially only friends, but in my dreams we'd live in the bush making our home from natural materials. We'd have about fourteen children, wear matching sarongs and live in the realm of love for the rest of our lives.

Bradley came back early. He'd been in a fight and was told to leave. I let him know

Kevin had been taking me out. Bradley said that was cool because all the money he earned was going on bills. I was hurt he didn't seem to care about my ex seeing me so I told him I'd let Kevin take me out again.

About a week later Bradley broke into my flat and took the letters he'd written me. I tried to act like I didn't care. That night he came over in the car he'd finally gotten on the road and was doing burnouts on the street outside. At one stage he came into my flat. Nick and Kevin were sitting on the couch, chatting. I asked Bradley if he wanted to sit down but he said no.

He walked outside and I followed. He told me to get in the car with him. Something about the way he spoke sent chills down my spine and I shook my head. I turned and ran back inside as Bradley drove off.

Not long after that Nick said he had to go, which was strange because after drinking he'd usually sleep on the couch. I was left alone with Kevin who didn't want to leave. I went to the bedroom to change into my bathrobe. Kevin came in and fell onto my bed, asking if he could just hold me. Uneasy about what Bradley was doing, I allowed myself to be held.

Just then there was a screeching of tyres outside and I knew Bradley was back. I ran to the window and there he was striding across the road towards me. I knew he wouldn't want to see Kevin there so I opened the window and called out, 'I'm busy right now.'

He stopped, turned around, walked back to his vehicle and opened the boot. He pulled out a big jerry can and splashed something over the car. While he was doing that I moved to the door. As I opened it, I thought he was trying to trick me to make me run over and declare my love for him. He was always playing practical jokes so I hesitated.

He jumped into the car, slammed the door, poured the substance over himself and struck a match. There was a massive explosion that lit the sky and shook the windows.

I knew I must have been in shock because this horror was burning my eyes, my heart and my soul. Time expanded as Bradley was silhouetted in the flames and I could not move. There was a dreadful noise louder than the raging inferno and I realized I was screaming. Not like I'd ever screamed before. This scream did not even hurt my throat. It was a terrible sound of unimaginable anguish and it came from a place deep inside I wasn't even aware of. My cells felt like they were changing, dissolving, and the blood froze in my veins.

Bradley was still burning before my eyes and in desperation I called out to Kevin. He'd been turned away as if he didn't want to see. At my call he ran out the door and straight to the car. I left my body, my vision was from up in the air and I saw I'd somehow made it to the road. He pulled Bradley from the vehicle and laid him on the asphalt.

He was still burning so Kevin ripped my dressing gown off and used it to try and beat out the flames. I was nude in the glare of lights and strangers were holding me back. Neighbours helped me to my flat to get some clothes on as Bradley was rushed away in an ambulance.

At the hospital Kevin's burnt hands were being bandaged and I was just standing there as the police were questioning us. They stopped when Bradley, behind a nearby curtain managed to whisper, 'My God, what have I done? I've killed myself!'

He was placed in an induced coma and taken to intensive care.

I was alone in the darkened reception area at the hospital. Knowing the olds wouldn't help, I called Carmel's number. She liked Bradley because of the time he stopped her de facto from harming her. Jed answered the phone, cursing that it was late. I told him Bradley had blown himself up and I wanted to talk to my sister. He snarled, '*I'm not waking her for this!*' And the line went dead.

The next few days were hell. I visited Bradley every day. His bloated, skinless frame was laid out, body fluids dripping on the floor. I told him how much I loved him, that he'd be alright and I'd be there to help him. I assured him everyone missed him and were all looking forward to seeing him. I was let in even though I was obviously not a relative. The nursing staff asked where his relatives were because Bradley needed the encouragement of visitors.

I ran into the girl he was staying with when I met him and told her Bradley needed a visit. She was unsure, but she came, and when she saw him she could not speak. Her eyes filled with tears and she left the room. Outside, she said she should not have come; she wanted to remember him as he was.

She told me the story of how she tried to make him jealous one night by bringing home another man. His response was to make them breakfast in bed the next morning! I recalled how I told him my sister was being bashed by her partner so he bought fresh peaches for her. While we were there Jed called her to come downstairs where he was drinking. We were left standing in their dining area when we heard Carmel scream in fear and Jed yelling. We moved to the window to see him threatening her with an axe. Bradley immediately jumped out the window and placed himself between them. No wonder Carmel adored him, as did anyone who'd been helped by his presence. So I took her to visit him and she tried to keep on talking, her eyes filled with horror.

To see what he'd done to himself was a torture I would never recover from. Why had he done that in front of me? Was it because he knew how much I cared and did that because of what Clara had done to him? As I had talked about suicide in the past, was he showing me how to do it?

Bradley's brothers organized a kind of party in his honour. Before I went I sat down and wrote out a prayer. It felt like automatic writing because I could hardly dress myself let alone write anything, but the prayer was a page long. I stopped in to see Bradley and asked the nurse if it was ok to read it to him. I can't remember all I had written but one line I could not forget – *Please let God help you. He would not have made you so beautiful if he did not love you so very much.*

When I arrived at his brothers' house I told them what hospital staff told me, that a visit would be welcome. They said they'd go the next day. I got home at about 2.30 am really out of it and crashed onto the bed, asleep. 3.00 am I sat straight up, wide awake as an icy wind blew through me.

'Bradley!' I called his name, feeling his presence.

I couldn't go back to sleep and as soon as Carmel arrived we went to the hospital. I asked to see Bradley and the nurse said, 'Wait a minute.'

A minute later the nurse came back. In her hand was a box of tissues. 'I'm sorry,' she said. 'Bradley died about 3.00 am.'

I crumpled to the floor as Carmel grabbed a handful of tissues. I was crying so hard I could barely walk. I asked her to take me to the hospital chapel where I collapsed on a pew, weeping. The priest arrived and said because Bradley committed suicide he wouldn't go to heaven. I tried to make him understand that Bradley had displayed qualities precious to the Lord. He was kind and caring, gentle and patient. He treated others with respect. His spirit was eternal. I could not believe the Lord would cast away such a precious soul.

The priest helped me to the street and I went home. I was looking after Kevin; he couldn't do much with his burnt hands heavily bandaged. He took one look at my face and knew Bradley was dead.

It was such a beautiful day I could not stay inside. Kevin helped me to the park where I lay on the ground and stared at the sky, tears streaming down my face. The Lord spoke to me then. He said Bradley was safe in His arms. That's great for him I thought; but what about me? How could I live now?

His shocking murder by his own hand killed my hopes and dreams. To have been able to share love with a man I could see Jesus in would have been everything to me. He was also a good looking, well-built, outstanding human being who amazed others with his kindness.

I dressed with great care for Bradley's funeral and chose a black satin, long-sleeved blouse and matching long skirt with silver bag and heels. I was determined to attend despite people blaming me because he suicided in front of me. Kevin and Nick helped me towards the chapel.

Bradley's ex came strutting towards me and her choice of attire seemed an affront. She was wearing an oversized black suit with a big yellow flower in the lapel. She looked like a clown to me. What was worse was the bitchy smirk on her face as she addressed me.

'You don't think he killed himself over you, do you?'

I looked straight into her eyes as I said coldly, 'No; I don't.'

***

A few days later Bradley's mum asked to see me and shook her head at my dishevelled appearance, saying I used to take such good care of myself. She said I could have anything of his I wanted. I chose a flannelette shirt he'd worn often and a piece of woven material that had adorned his dressing table.

It would be easy to blame his broken, dysfunctional family or his ex. Yet he had the grace to rise above depravity through excellent manners, kindness and service to others. I remembered one day his mother was due to visit so he set a beautiful table for her and served her tea. He did the same for my parents and I was put out at the time. How could he be so gracious to people who destroyed my life?

Deep down I knew; I played a part in his death.

The Lord blessed me with recognition of the brilliant light of Bradley's soul and I mishandled my part. Through fear and lack of self-esteem, I held back my love.

I was sure I'd have love and fulfilment as an adult. I'd just turned twenty-two and my life was over. The shock and horror of what Bradley did in front of me was the end of me. The unbearable grief and anguish were etched into my face for all to see.

For the first time in my life I wore dark sunglasses. No amount of alcohol or drugs could even ease the pain that consumed me. There was no escape in sleep either; I'd wake to a pillow wet with tears. There was no alternative, I had to die.

I became homeless and wandered the streets, crying. Kind strangers offered shelter or a meal and in a way that was so sad because I should have been able to have support from relatives. Of course, they were nowhere to be found.

My sisters actually sat around making up jokes and laughing about it.

'Did you hear some guy threw himself in front of a train last night?'

'Yeah, he must have gone out with Paula – ha ha.'

One lady said I could stay at her house. I didn't know she was tight with a bike gang. The first night a naked guy burst into my room and told me to have sex with him and the woman. I was asleep and angry at being woken by sleaze so I told the guy to *get out*!

His voice was menacing as he said softly, 'You're going to pay for this!'

The next morning, biker moles were in the kitchen with the sleazebag, who ordered them to get rid of me. I ran to the phone box, called the old boy and begged him to come and get me. He said no at first. I told him the moles were throwing my clothes out the window and were coming to bash me if I didn't leave pronto. He complained but said he'd be there soon. He showed up just in time as I was gathering up the discarded rags they hadn't stolen.

The old boy drove to the other side of town, pulled up in front of a boarding house for down and out men, gave me fifty dollars and drove away. It was humiliating to be the only woman staying with winos even though they were polite to me.

Realization came slowly that I was too gutless to take my own life but I had to keep trying. If I had to live I'd have to find a way to support myself but how could I? I couldn't stop crying because my heart was not only broken, it was torched and detonated into burnt and bleeding pieces that could never be healed.

I allowed myself to feel bitter. There was no hope of love for me now. If I couldn't die I'd have to make money somehow. Guys were always trying to have sex with me so maybe I'd make them pay for the privilege. I actually went to a brothel early one morning and was warmly received. I'd be welcome if I chose that path. I knew selling my body was a sin. I envisioned the reality of the position, pretending to be intimate with strangers and felt physically ill. I knew I could never do that.

Amy, the girl who stayed at the olds for a while, was dancing at a club in the Valley. She explained that the set-up was unique and working there was an easy way to earn money. The Purple Parrott was an adult amusement arcade featuring such distractions as Dunk the Dolly, Girly Go Round, Body Painting, Peep Shows and Private Dancers. Patrons were not allowed to touch. Drugs and security were provided. This job seemed more suitable. I'd been told my dancing was sensual and I loved dressing in silky lingerie. All I had to do was learn a spiel, carefully worded so the punters thought they may get sex – which of course they didn't. Any girl caught having sex was instantly dismissed. There was a brothel next door if they preferred that sort of employment.

I had preconceived ideas of the sort of women who worked at 'The Parrott' and assumed they would be hardened sluts but I was wrong. Only a few of them were there strictly for money. Most were beautiful, but broken like me.

The Parrott was an alluring attraction at night. Spruikers outside herded drunken strays into the dark interior lit with disco lighting and the scantily clad women would explain the various activities and their cost.

Some of the girls were really nice and lots of fun. To work there was a lifestyle because after closing we'd hit the clubs and dance till dawn. Home for a few hours sleep and out to a poker game, pub session or other social gathering. One girl, Amber, was the daughter of a high ranking policeman. She complained about the disabled who frequented The Parrott because she said they always chose her and made her feel uncomfortable. One night a severely disabled man was wheeled in and nodded at her. She turned to me and whispered, 'See! I told you, Cherry! Please come in with me!' (Cherry was a nickname I chose for my stage name.)

The disabled guy asked for a Body Paint and we entered the body paint room. The disabled man's carer placed a brush in his mouth and held the palette up for him. The man in the wheelchair loaded the brush with red paint, and with his teeth, drew it slowly across Amber's throat. She screamed, jumped up and ran from the room while I leaned against the wall, laughing helplessly.

I moved in with Lace and a girl who worked at the brothel. The girls asked why I was alone. I told them the man I loved had died and they said they understood. They were sure I should have sex though and tried to hook me up with various males. I wasn't interested but appreciated their concern.

Dressing for work one night I stopped and looked in the mirror. I appeared as a caricature of my former self. A cheap and brassy imitation of the natural lady I was. I went to the kitchen and took hold of a large knife. Turning back to the mirror I held the blade to my throat. Tears were streaking the makeup down my cheeks as I sneered to my reflection, 'Go on, you gutless bitch! Do it!' But I couldn't!

I hadn't worked there long when my leg became too sore to dance on. The pain was deep and I knew whatever was causing it was killing me. I felt relief and went to stay at Rita's where drugs and alcohol were plentiful. All I had to do was endure the pain until I was dead.

After a few days I was limping and couldn't sleep because of the constant agony. One morning mother walked in and said, 'Your face is black. I'm taking you to hospital.'

I was too defeated to argue. The old girl dropped me at the emergency entrance and left. Doctors couldn't determine the cause of pain. Morphine had taken the edge off but I could still feel it. The next morning, tests revealed Deep Vein Thrombosis. Further tests showed the coagulation was extensive and I was hospitalized for weeks.

Upon release from hospital two of my nephew's friends approached me and asked if I had his new address. I said I didn't know the name of the street but knew how to get there. They made arrangements to pick me up that evening. James and Ryan arrived in a sports car.

James accelerated and lost control of the vehicle. His car left the road and flew through the air. The stereo was blaring out rock music and I knew we were going to crash. A fog seemed to be rolling into my vision blocking out everything, until there was nothing but blackness.

Regaining consciousness, my eyes opened to bright lights and firemen telling me it was ok, they were going to get me out. They had to cut the roof to free me from the wreck and I was rushed by ambulance to hospital.

A nurse informed me that both young men died almost instantly from their injuries. I was spared. It was as if the Lord was telling me to stop praying to die. For now I had to live but I didn't want to! I survived that horror childhood for this? I was angry at God and told him I would do nothing. How could I possibly go on? I was more destroyed than ever. As He wanted me to live, He could give me something to live for.

Through all these experiences, the Lord had been preparing me to rise up to the next level.

Paula Rule

Glory of Love

You must be holy for I am Holy. 1 Peter 1:16

A few weeks later a friend called and said an acquaintance wanted to meet me. The man spoke briefly on the phone and made his intentions clear. He said he'd seen me walking past his workshop and knew I was the one for him.

I told him to come over straight away as there was a group of us there. He arrived on a Harley and I looked him over. His faded blue jeans, black leather jacket and boots were well worn and well cared for. He was slim and muscular with shoulder length silky black hair and clean, tanned skin. As he introduced himself I noticed his hazel eyes and knockout smile. He said his name was Chris Rule. Even his name was cool!

Chris was a good looking guy and totally down to earth. He was hard working and his extensive knowledge of various trades meant he could make money doing almost anything. He'd recently opened his own panel beating business because he knew his work was of the highest standard. The house he was renting was old and rundown but he'd fixed a lot of things there.

He asked me to go with him for a weekend at the Gold Coast. This trip would show me if he was a sleaze but from the moment he picked me up in a rental car I felt safe and happy. We went to nightclubs on the strip at Surfers and the next morning we had breakfast at the casino. Chris only held my hand or placed his hand on my back to guide me through the crowds so I knew I could trust him.

The early months with him were magic. Chris was so kind and gentle and would leave his work to visit me. One day he surprised me by taking me to the area where I grew up. We enjoyed a leisurely drive around the mountain and at one point he stopped the car by the side of the road and led me into the bush.

We walked for a short distance and he sat me down on a natural rock seat by a waterfall. I spent my childhood here and often explored the area but had never seen this waterfall before. I was totally blown away! Chris took my hand, smiled into my eyes and asked me to marry him. I didn't want to appear too eager so I said, 'We'll see.'

I knew I was glowing with love and happiness and he could see it. He then asked me to move in with him and I said yes. That first night in his bed he looked deeply into my eyes and told me he was giving me his baby.

Living with Chris was great. He was clean, tidy and could make or fix pretty well everything. He'd get out of bed about 6.00 am straight into his work clothes and stayed at his workshop all day to come home about 6.00 pm for dinner. Before he met me he practically lived at that shed!

I cleaned the old, rundown house he was renting and cut flowers from the heavy jasmine vine that hung over the fence. I placed them in vases so a lovely fragrance would help to welcome my man home. I'd never felt so contented, natural and carefree.

Chris often helped with dinner and then we'd relax in front of the TV. On the weekends he was building a car for me. I served him cold drinks and sandwiches, admiring the play of muscles across his tanned arms and back, his hair shining in the sun. I'd sit on the steps and watch him work, in awe of his skill and ability. He'd be smiling up at me with that expression that said he was completely happy. I felt exactly the same way.

When I moved in, Chris told the woman he left two years before he met me to apply for their divorce, so we could be married.

Morning sickness was a twenty-four hour a day event and I always had a bucket handy to vomit in. I was four months pregnant when Chris had a seizure in the shower. Hearing a loud crash I ran in to see him frothing at the mouth; face bleeding, body contorting on the floor. Terrified, I rang an ambulance and the attendants asked if he was on drugs. Chris came out of it and refused to go to the hospital. He said he'd be fine.

As the weeks passed Chris began to experience crippling headaches when the pain extended to the back of his neck. He blew his nose and what came out was black. I convinced him to have a doctor come to the house. His diagnosis was that the condition was psychosomatic. Another physician was summoned and he said it was probably just stress. After he left, Chris just shook his head and said, 'I told you babe, they just don't care.'

The next morning Chris wouldn't look me in the eye. His back was towards me when he said over his shoulder, 'I want you to leave.'

I could not believe what I was hearing. Was his love just an act? Was my heart going to be broken again? I started to get angry, the old coping mechanism from childhood. My voice had an edge when I spoke.

'What do you mean?' I cried. 'What have I done wrong?'

But Chris was like stone. 'I asked you to leave.'

Tears were pouring down my face. 'I'll only leave if you say you don't love me.'

He still wouldn't face me. 'Ok, I don't love you, now go.'

I went to pack my few things, telling him I was worried about him, that I wanted to look after him. He responded by throwing stones as I ran from the property.

The old boy dropped me at an institution for unmarried mothers. It was cold and sterile, the staff uncaring. I felt humiliated, sick and worried about Chris. At every opportunity I tried to call him but there was no answer. After two days I became so worried I knew I had to leave. On entry to that place I'd signed a document literally signing away my life to the institution until the birth of my child.

I rang the old boy and told him Chris was sick and needed me. I told him when to come, where to park – and to keep the engine running. I chose a time when the more relaxed manageress was on. As I was throwing my suitcase in the boot she hurried over.

'Where do you think you're going? You are not allowed to leave this property!'

I slammed the boot shut and strode to the passenger door. 'Try and stop me or get out of my way.' My voice was hard as I jumped in the car.

I was dropped off outside Chris's house and slowly went up the stairs, not knowing what to expect.

The place was in disarray and Chris was lying on his bed, he looked very ill. As I rushed to his side I knew, I loved Chris the same way I loved Bradley; eternally. I stroked his hair back and kissed him. He looked relieved to see me and asked why I was there. As I was straightening the bedclothes and making him more comfortable I said, 'I'll stay until you're well, then if you still don't want me, I'll go.'

'I didn't want to be a burden to you,' he said. 'I know how sick you are with the pregnancy.'

Two days later I awoke to Chris hanging backwards off the bed, frothing at the mouth, having a full-on fit. I knew he was against seeing a doctor but I couldn't take much more of this. I wrote down all the symptoms he'd exhibited and took him to hospital. I handed the note to a nurse and told her to read it. We were led to an examination room in the emergency department and were left alone for a few minutes. Chris and I held hands in silence before he spoke, 'I can see double, babe.' He sounded so vulnerable that I was quick to reassure him. We'd tell the doctors we weren't leaving until they found out what was wrong.

Hours went by as I sat in the waiting area. Finally a doctor called my name. He said Chris was terminally ill with a malignant brain tumour and would have to be operated on as soon as a specialist surgeon could be summoned. If he made it through the operation he was not expected to live for more than two weeks, as a vegetable.

The doctor walked briskly away as the child convulsed in my womb. I felt deathly ill and didn't know what to do. I went in and saw Chris. They'd obviously told him because he was shaking so hard he could barely talk. He asked me to stay but I told him I had to go, that I'd be back in the morning.

I rang the old boy and asked him to come and get me. He took me to their house where they said Chris's estranged wife must be informed. I told them Chris didn't like her – he'd left her two years before he met me. They insisted as she was the mother of three of his children she had a right to know. Sick of their badgering I told them her address and they went straight to tell her. Through the long night I wondered what to do. Listening to my relatives laughing and drinking as I sat out on the front step alone, I knew the only person who loved me was Chris.

The next morning I was up early and made my way to the hospital. I walked over to Chris's bed and could see they were ready to take him to theatre.

'I'm here darling,' I said softly. 'I love you forever and I'm not going anywhere.'

In the waiting room I wondered what the outcome would be. Would he even make it through the surgery? Would he recognize me or remember our love? What about our baby? I was told Chris might not even know me because if he lived for a brief time he was expected to lose his short-term memory. Hours later I was informed he survived the operation.

Chris was in intensive care for the next three days. His mother had flown up from Sydney and expended her energy on his ex, Donna. I was left standing in hallways alone as the two women whispered to each other. They treated me like I did not exist.

I couldn't afford new maternity clothes and caught them sneering at my outdated, charity store dress. Stella actually spoke to me once, to say I should leave Chris and meet someone else who could raise the baby. They seemed as if they wanted to have Chris, and maybe together they would provide more for him than I could. I went in to speak with them. My heart was heavy as I said slowly, 'If you want Chris so much, you can have him.'

His mother glanced at me and said, 'We have him booked into Mt Olivett.'

I could not believe what I was hearing! Here they were making a big fuss over Chris but thought nothing of conveniently dumping him in an institution for the terminally ill. Completely disgusted I declared, 'Then you can't have him! If neither of you love Chris enough to take care of him, I'll fight you!'

I burst out crying as I ran clumsily down the hallway. I made it to the chapel, where three years before, I tried but failed to make sense of the tragic suicide of Bradley. Hiding my deep love for him had been the biggest mistake of my life. I vowed before God I would not make that same mistake now.

The chapel was deserted, quiet and peaceful. I prayed earnestly to the Lord, asking for guidance. I thought of Chris. What he would want. I knew he hated hospitals and would be horrified to wake up in an institution. I'd been looking after him anyway and knew I could provide the most important thing to Chris; real and true love.

I had a chance to give and share love now but I'd have to fight for it! I'd be vulnerable and exposed but I felt my whole life had led to this moment. I *had to be* what God created me to be, putting aside the tough façade my inner child to wanted wear now. During those sacred moments alone in the chapel, I prayed with all my heart I would succeed because I'd give my life to be with

Chris. I couldn't dwell on what he must be going through or what I was feeling. I would just focus on the love we shared.

Chris was transferred to a ward and I was shocked to see a large number of staples holding his swollen skull together. He was propped up, sweating profusely, trying not to topple onto the floor. There was food on his tray but it was out of his reach. I gently straightened him up and wiped the sweat from his brow. I sat beside him and started to feed him his lunch. He looked puzzled as I was talking to him.

'Chris, it's me, Paula. Don't you remember me?' He still looked unsure and I burst out crying. 'We live together – we love each other. Chris, I'm having your baby!' I took his hand and ran it over my swollen breasts and belly while tears ran down my cheeks. He looked stunned and overwhelmed so I kissed him with all the love and passion inside me. I kissed away my tears from his beautiful face. 'I'm going to take care of you my darling. Don't worry about anything. You just get well soon.' There was suddenly a deep feeling of intimacy between us as I continued to feed Chris his lunch and made sure he was comfortable.

From the time Chris was unable to work, creditors were banging on the door and bills were piling up. While he was hospitalized his workplace was broken into and stripped. That same night the thieves broke in under the house he rented. I lay on his cold waterbed shivering with fear. In the darkness I clutched a knife for protection, praying they wouldn't come upstairs. They took everything of value from under the house and even took the shell of the car he was making for me.

No one else was attending to his affairs so I reluctantly went through his papers and began opening his mail. He was evicted from that house and I had to move our few remaining belongings to a sister's ex-boyfriend's place, there was nowhere else to go. Every day I visited with Chris and every day our love grew stronger.

His condition improved and he was transferred to a small complex at the back of the hospital where they housed hopeless cases and people with Aids. One patient was a young woman named Heather. She had HIV, Hepatitis C and had fallen out a window shattering both her legs but she was the most outgoing person I'd met and it was impossible not to like her. She liked Chris and would often be sitting outside with him when I arrived. I could have been jealous that she was around him all the time but realized she would be there to talk with him when I couldn't.

It's true that people with a brain tumour can develop precognition. I was telling Chris how the ultra sound revealed our unborn child. Without missing a beat, Chris said, 'He's a boy and he'll be premature. You'll name him after me, won't you, love.

Chris wanted to come home straight away but I had to tell him we'd been evicted and I'd have to find us somewhere to live.

During this time a large envelope arrived for Chris. I noticed it was from the legal firm his ex was using. The bitch was stopping their divorce proceedings! She stated they spent three nights together at the hospital (yeah, when Chris was unconscious in intensive care!) and were reconciled. The document was full of lies. She swore she couldn't remember who told her about Chris's cancer – it was *my* damned parents! She said the tumour caused Chris to act in an antisocial manner and that's why they broke up! Chris told me he left her because he had no respect for her. I was disgusted she would do this to Chris when he was at his most vulnerable and hurt because she wouldn't have done it without Stella's backing. I rushed to the hospital to tell Chris. I was furious and told him when Donna showed up; I was going to deal with her.

Chris was calm. He held my hand and said, 'Please babe, let me handle it.'

When she entered the room I was standing beside Chris's bed, holding his hand. Out of respect for Chris I said nothing. There was silence for a moment.

Chris said, 'I heard you've taken legal action against me.'

She replied, 'Yes, I have.'

Chris spoke quietly, but firmly and clearly. 'Then I never want to see you again.'

I contacted a legal firm on Chris's behalf so he could strengthen his legal position. I waited outside while lawyers drew up a will from his instructions. He made his will in contemplation of our marriage and took legal steps to stop Donna having anything to do with us. He even stated that he left her nothing due to her terrible treatment.

Chris was a lot more relaxed after he made his will but I didn't trust his ex at all. I approached people who had contact with him before he became ill and they wrote out sworn statements that he was a great person who'd never been anti-social. He was my man and we planned to marry.

Chris and I could not just get married. Because of the diagnosis that he was a dying vegetable he had to get permission from his cancer specialist. Chris and I were interviewed separately and together. Doctor Quinlan was happy for us. He told me he'd never seen such dignity as Chris possessed or the depth of love we shared.

Christmas was coming up so I went to the city to buy gifts. I bought us both a chain, his with his birth sign, mine with a small gold heart. It would be our first Christmas together. I spent every day at the hospital and catering staff began giving me unclaimed meals so Chris and I could eat together.

Then it was New Year's Eve. I walked to the service station near the hospital to buy some munchies to share with Chris. The girl behind the counter knew Chris and asked how he was. I told her I was on my way to spend the evening with him. She said I could take anything from the shop I wanted, she would pay for it. I grabbed some chips, lollies and two ice creams. Her kindness touched my heart and tears filled my eyes as I thanked her.

***

Rental accommodation was hard to find as the agents always asked about my partner's employment. When I told them my man was terminally ill, they said no. Chris got tired of waiting and tried to sign himself out. He was sitting outside in a wheelchair, his stuff piled up on his lap. He looked so determined yet so vulnerable that I had to smile.

'Where are you off to?' I asked.

'You're taking me home.'

'We don't have a home yet babe; I'm still working on it. But I promise you, we will soon.'

I helped him put his things away and knew *somehow* I'd have to secure a place for us to live. I rang about a flat and took Rita's ex with me to see it. The owner assumed the man I was with was my boyfriend and said I could have it. He looked surprised to see Chris there when he came to get the rent but said nothing.

Chris responded well to radium treatment and was offered chemotherapy. He didn't want chemo but was persuaded to try it. I assured him if he didn't like it he wouldn't have to do it again. When I went to get him at the end of his first session, he'd tried to dress himself and was sitting on the bed in his own excrement. I gently led him to the showers; washed him, dried him off, dressed him and took him home. He refused to go back for more and that was cool by me.

Chris was forced to file for bankruptcy and I had to push him in a wheelchair through the main streets of the city to do so. Tears ran down my cheeks to see him try to sign his name, both of us knowing if he hadn't become ill this wouldn't be happening.

He insisted on helping with chores even when half his body felt numb. He could not see very well since the operation but that didn't stop him going to the local shop alone. I knew his independence was everything to him, so I gave him money and a note and watched from the top of the hill as he made his way unsteadily to the shop. I'd keep watch until I could see him making his way back and would be waiting inside when he returned.

We began planning our wedding. Chris wanted us married as soon as possible and we set the date, 9th February, 1991.

Unexpectedly, my water broke. The hospital wouldn't allow Chris to be present for the birth. They said that as his carer I wouldn't be able to look after him during labour. My sisters said when the time came one of them would look after him while I had the baby. On the day they all said they were busy, so I sat there for hours refusing to go to hospital until I knew Chris would have someone there. Finally Karen said she would watch him.

I was exhausted from looking after Chris and dozed through most of the birth. Our son arrived six days before our wedding and eight weeks premature. My legs were still numb from the epidural when my sister rushed in, left Chris and ran out without even asking about the baby. I had to wait hours until I could walk again to take him home.

We were on government benefits and money was tight so we bought the cheapest rings we could find. Our wedding day arrived. Chris wore his good shirt and jeans and I wore a second hand maternity dress from a charity. A florist who heard about us donated the flowers I held and wore in my hair.

Before the ceremony I briefly imagined the sort of wedding most women dream of; a stunning gown, huge glittering ring, a healthy male who could share love for a lifetime. Chris had not been able to make love to me since he became ill and many people told me I was crazy to marry a man who was bankrupt, dying and could not even hold me or see me properly.

The days passed and were bright with love. To be Chris's wife was an honour. Every moment was special because we never knew if it would be our last. We may not have been able to make love but our every touch was all about love.

We made preparations to baptize our son and I asked Chris when he'd been baptized. He said he'd never been baptized but wanted to be.

'You love Jesus, don't you?'

'Yes I do,' he replied.

'Trust in Jesus is all you need. When the priest arrives just tell him you want a deeper friendship with Jesus. That's all you have to do.' We arranged to have the ceremony at home. During Easter, Father Michael officiated and baptized my family.

We kept in contact with Heather and her boyfriend and would meet them at the pub for a few drinks. We went to a friend's wedding where guests asked if Chris had been in a car accident. Stella asked him to fly down and visit with her and Chris wanted to go. He was confident she'd give him one thousand dollars to buy a car. When we brought our son home, I let him go to her.

On the day of his return I was so excited I got to the airport two hours early. When Chris came into view I burst into happy tears to see my man home safe. He had the money in his wallet and told the cab driver to take us to a car yard not far away. Chris asked the sales person if they had a cheap Ford. He directed the guy to start the vehicle and listened to the engine. That's how he chose our car.

We applied for public housing and because of Chris's condition we were offered a place almost immediately but in an outlying shire. Chris wanted that, he said he couldn't stand the thought of people who knew him, staring at him.

The duplex was new and had no floor or window coverings. We hung sheets and blankets over the windows and someone found some old carpet for us. We used packing boxes for tables and lived a quiet life at home. Every day our love grew stronger. We could feel the presence and approval of the Lord. It was like He was recording our love for His private stash.

Chris began to lose mobility. I carried him around for a while because he refused to sit in the wheelchair again. My health was deteriorating too so he refused to get out of bed. When the baby was asleep I'd lie down beside Chris and listen as he told me about his life. Years later I shared these stories with our son.

I usually woke around dawn to feel Chris's warmth beside me. I'd reach out and run my hand down his side. Some mornings I'd just lie there quietly and watch his eyes open. At first his eyes would widen with that *am I alive?* look. Then he'd realize he was safe with me and visibly relax. The momentary look of panic and fear, replaced with eyes overflowing with love for me. I would spend those precious minutes caressing and kissing my man. The days were filled with endless chores I had to do. The washing machine broke down so I just hand washed. I was giving everything I had with all my heart. I was exhausted, but fulfilled. I never dreamed I could be so happy.

The supplier of incontinence pads stated in a letter they wouldn't bring more to the house. I penned a reply to the company and as I cried I wrote that I'd put my husband in our son's nappies if they wouldn't deliver. Two days later I received a call from a woman at the company. She was crying and assured me the pads would arrive directly. They left us three boxes. By this time Chris was finding it hard to keep food down and I didn't feel like eating when he couldn't.

On the fourteenth of March, 1992 we awoke as usual. I'd just finished bathing and dressing Chris when he started breathing heavily. I held him in my arms, calling his name. My heart was beating so hard I could not discern if he was breathing. The next phase was supposed to be a coma. I ran to the phone to call the doctor who'd been coming every week to check on Chris. He wasn't there but I insisted someone come at once, there was something wrong!

Finally some guy arrived, glanced into the bedroom and said, 'Oh yeah, he's dead.'

His casual assumption upset me. 'Well, could you please check, because if he is I have to call the funeral home.'

He went into the bedroom and sat by Chris for a minute. 'Yes, he's dead. Now tell me your story, I heard about you two down at the surgery.'

'*Get out*!!' was all I could say.

When he was gone I rang the funeral parlour and they informed me they'd arrive in an hour. I went to Chris and slowly lay down beside him. No need to rush around anymore. He smelled so clean and appeared to be merely asleep. Tears fell from my eyes as I kissed his lips and held him close; one last time.

Time moved forward and so soon they came and put my Chris in a body bag and took him away. Everyone else was expecting it but I wasn't. I hoped the Lord would let him live, for his son and me. I was too grief-stricken to see it then but God had already performed a miracle. He had given us time to enjoy life to the full. Chris didn't die on the operating table and was more of a man than anyone I've ever known. Right up to the moment of his death he displayed more wisdom than the doctors who labelled him a 'vegetable'.

I had to arrange his funeral on my twenty-seventh birthday. It was important to me not to cry at the service. I wanted to display the dignity Chris possessed and my faith that he was home with the Lord. I dressed with care and chose to read a lovely prayer. Stella asked for an open casket and that enabled me to place a dozen red roses on his chest. He looked so handsome, so innocent. He would now be forever young, just like Bradley.

Those who supported me were on one side of the church and Chris's relatives on the other. During the service we were to give each other a sign of peace but his relatives just stood there. I walked over to them and one by one I shook their hands or embraced them. They were stiff and unwelcoming but the important thing was that I forgave them. On that day I forgave my relatives and even felt sorry for them.

At the cemetery we stood around his grave and I didn't want to leave. One by one the others departed and I was alone with Chris for the last time. As I looked up to the sky I felt a gentle hand on my shoulder and a voice from heaven said, 'Well done, My daughter.' Those eternal moments feeling the approval of the Lord made all my suffering valid and worthwhile. I knew Chris was safe in heaven. He had graduated this consciousness with honours.

I'd been greatly blessed to share true love with such a worthy person. Another whole chapter of my life was over. Chris sought me out when I had nothing and left me with so much to be grateful for. He brought out the best in me. His courage inspired me. His love completed me. He even left me with a reason to live, to love and care for his son.

Stella loudly stated at the service that she would contribute to the cost of her son's funeral. When I rang her to ask how much she would put in, she was cold.

'I'm not giving you a red cent,' she sneered.

'Then burn in hell!' I felt bad speaking like that but she had betrayed her son for the last time. Others warned me not to have anything to do with Stella. They said she hated me and would find a way to hurt me. They were right. I knew then I had no relatives to call on from either side.

I was able to pay for his funeral with insurance money from the car accident I survived.

Chris's love enabled me to live despite deep grief. Now I'd always grieve for him too. Bradley had taken his life away but Chris chose to live with love and trust. I was left feeling as fragile as spun glass. Both of the men I loved eternally were gone from this life forever. At night I'd drive up to the mountains with my baby and look out to the stars. I was so tired, so worn out. I really didn't want to go on but I had a responsibility and needed to be strong enough to see it through no matter what. I had a child to raise – alone.

God provided strength I didn't have and I was able to continue. I put a deposit on an old house through a government loan, a home–share loan. This meant we didn't really own the house but could not be kicked out as long as I made the payments and maintained the property. The residence was centrally located between where Chris and I had lived and the church where his funeral mass was held. The agent neglected to tell me the area was the worst in the shire.

I adored our son and my whole life was to care for him. People on the street called me 'smiley' as I was always smiling. I thought God would bring me a partner to share love and help raise my baby. The years passed and my anticipation faded.

Widows are described in the Bible as vulnerable people abused by society. I live the reality and it's true. I've been bashed and raped, my doors and windows kicked in by violent men. I was targeted by paedophiles wanting to abuse my son. Hypocrites pretended to like me while scheming to use me. Other women looked down on me or were cruel because I had no man to back me up. Trades people overcharged or did a poor job and threatened me if I complained.

Our house became more and more run down. I went without food, new clothes and a car (the old Ford finally died) to keep the roof over my son's head, food in his mouth and clothes on his back. I felt a sacred duty to provide my child with a devoted mum and chose to be there for him full time. Maybe I should have had a permanent job but being there for him was priceless. We'd have picnics in the back yard and read stories together. We'd go to the park and the beach and he called me the best mum in the world.

Unexpected bills or expenses meant I'd have to apply for charity. Charitable institutions seemed to choose the most obnoxious people to assess eligibility for assistance. I'd come away from them weeping with shame.

Asking the olds for help was just as bad. I had to beg and weep so they'd deposit five dollars in my account. They sold their beachfront property and bought vehicles and cosmetic surgery for their favourites amongst my sisters. I wrote to them quoting scripture stating they should be the ones to help me. I asked them for a car. They responded with a letter stating they wouldn't give me anything. My son came home from school that day to see tears streaming down my face. I could not speak. He saw the letter in my hand and didn't even look at it; just ripped it up and threw it in the bin. What was the point of forgiving those people when they continued to treat me so badly? They never asked for my forgiveness and didn't offer assistance either.

The only personal life I had was my sacred memories. Most evenings after my child was asleep I'd sit on the couch and weep, aching with loneliness and grief.

As my son got older he asked me to give him a dad. I told him he has a dad who's in heaven watching over us but he wanted someone physically there and I tried to meet someone. I went out on dates but knew I couldn't be with any of them. My husband left me with a very high standard that needed to be fulfilled. I became disheartened. All my love was not enough for my son. I knew he appreciated me but he felt he needed a male role model.

I thought God would bring a partner into my life if that was His plan and prayed for that every night. As much joy as I felt raising my son, I was enduring for him and my eternal soul.

At one stage I tried a physical relationship with a man who was otherwise unsuitable (he told me he was a woodchopper and a single man but I found out he was a career criminal who already had a mistress!). He was a good lover and I attained a momentary physical satisfaction but was left feeling even more bereft and alone than before.

One day my son and I were sitting in the waiting area of a doctors' surgery. I released a deep sigh, contemplating the rest of my life alone with only memories for company, when I looked up, straight into the eyes of a stranger.

Paula Rule

Ecstasy of Spirit

The Holy Spirit within you has seen your brother and recognized him perfectly since time began. ACIM

Time stood still for what seemed an eternity. It was like gazing into a mirror of God's perfect love for me. I'd never experienced anything like that before. A *stranger* was the portal to my instant ecstasy of spirit? In his eyes I saw my eternal beauty of soul created by the Lord. Why should I feel that way about a *doctor*? Those types proved to be incompetent and uncaring to my husband and they hadn't treated me that well either. Later, I learned his name was Paul King.

I instantly assumed he was married and therefore none of my business. So how could this stranger have such an effect on me? Even though nothing was said, I felt he was just as blown away by me as I was by him. But it seemed ridiculous! I learned no one could compare to the precious memories I cherished. I tried to forget the powerful feelings he evoked in me so I could get on with my life.

I'd been widowed for years when I heard my Aunt Rose had died. Both our husbands succumbed to cancer and that was when we became friends. She lived in a lovely house on the river and her wish was to stay in her home until she died.

It was not to be. She had adult children who sent police to break in to her house and take her to institutionalized care. Her tenant rang to tell me she'd been dragged, kicking and screaming from her home.

I begged a ride from people to visit her and whenever I walked into the room she would say, 'Paula, Paula Rule.' She knew me straight away even though she was labelled as demented.

She ended up in a good facility where they were kind to her but her heart was broken. She asked me to take her away from there and I had to say I couldn't, her children were in charge of her.

The day she died I threw on some shorts and a top and took my son to the park. It was deserted except for a man and a small boy.

The little boy came running up to me and said, 'Are you my mummy? Can you please be my mummy?'

He was adorable and my heart melted. He said his name was Jamie and he dragged me over to the man. Chris and Jamie ran off to play. Jamie's dad introduced himself as Kyle. He appeared to be good looking but didn't remove his dark sunglasses. The way he kept looking me up and down then around the deserted park made me nervous and I shivered. I called to Chris that we had to leave. He asked if we could go to their place after lunch and I agreed.

Later that day we arrived at their home. Chris and Jamie played all afternoon and I accepted the offer to stay for dinner. The kids were tired and went for a nap. Kyle seemed alright and poured me a glass of wine. Not long after that he said he was going to the toilet. Next thing, he came running out stark naked, knocked me down and pinned me to the floor. I struggled but he was too strong. I kept saying no but he just laughed at my refusal of what he was inflicting on me.

All the years I'd valued my celibacy were brutally ignored. My feeling of personal safety was gone. Determined not to wake the children I didn't scream. As soon as he finished he jumped up and so did I. I could not contain my fury and was quietly swearing he was going to pay for what he did to me. I ran around stuffing our things in my bag so I could get my child and go. Kyle went ballistic.

He ripped the phone out of the wall so I couldn't call for help. He said he was going to kill us. The horror was just beginning and I can only remember images of what happened next. He grabbed his son and threw him against the wall. The child was screaming hysterically as his father was punching him in the head.

Somehow Chris and I made it outside and so did the monster. He put a cigarette out on his boy's face. We were screaming and all I wanted to do was get home but I was frozen by his shocking abuse. On the street, a car went slowly past. The occupants of the vehicle must have seen there was something wrong because a woman called out.

I looked up into the rapist's face. He was pretending to smile to make out that everything was alright. His eyes were black holes that chilled me to the bone. I took Chris's hand, ran all the way home and locked us inside.

The phone rang through the night. I answered once to hear him saying I'd be dead if I told anyone what he'd done. The next morning the little boy rang, calling me mummy and asking me to come over. I knew I was putting myself and my son in danger but I could not refuse him.

I knew if I reported the rape Kyle would blame me. I'd never encountered a male so obviously on the edge. I felt I had no choice but to try and help him. I expressed my shock and horror at his actions and let him know my feeling of personal safety was gone.

I felt sick and soon learned I was pregnant. I didn't want to have an abortion but didn't want to carry the foetus of a child-bashing rapist either. My son was worried when he saw I was sick so I told him the truth of my condition and what I thought I should do.

Chris said no. 'Don't kill my little brother! If you do I'll never forgive you!'

I hadn't been able to find a dad for him and didn't want him to ever be able to say I murdered his brother. I decided the child was a gift from God and no matter how difficult it was to be pregnant alone, Chris would have a brother.

During the pregnancy I began to see Dr King regularly. I was sure he assumed I had a partner, and though I told him the baby was 'pushed onto me' he did not associate that with rape. Because this man affected me so deeply I didn't want him to see me as a victim. It seemed crazy but every time I saw him I was overwhelmed with pure love.

One day he gently stroked his fingers across my hand and it was a perfect moment. I blushed and looked away because I was suddenly blinded by fireworks that seemed to be going off all around me. In that instant I was Cinderella, Snow White and every fairytale princess I ever heard of. I can hardly remember anything I've said to him as all my energy went into trying to act cool and sound coherent.

An ex neighbour said she would stay for the birth and her mother would look after Chris. In the delivery room a nurse asked where the father was. I told her what happened to me and she said she'd write that in my chart. I said no as the rapist threatened to kill me if I named him.

When Kyle heard I was going to have the baby he left the area. He was still threatening me over the phone so I told him I had to inform the authorities about what he'd done to me and his son. I also let him know a friend wanted to get revenge for me. I stressed I did not reveal his name and never would as long as he left me alone.

After the birth government officials asked for statements to attest to the rape. I knew I told Dr King the child had been pushed on to me so I made an appointment to see him. I took Chris with me as he witnessed the abuse of the child after I was attacked. As I sat in the waiting area I prayed I'd be able to clearly explain what happened. It never occurred to me that he might not believe me.

He came out into the waiting area and pushed my baby's pram into the consultation room. I tried to explain that I'd been raped. He exploded with anger and said no, he didn't remember me saying the child had been pushed onto me. He didn't even give me a chance to tell him the details of what happened! His reaction left me feeling violated all over again and I left.

I saw him a few times after that to show I was sincere but his energy was cold and closed. I tried to think of a way to get through to him and wrote him a letter. I hoped he would read it and realize I was not that kind of person. He was paid to be my doctor not my judge.

After I knew he would have received my letter, I entered the surgery and he was standing behind the receptionist. He was blushing and smiling at me. I felt my own cheeks flush and looked away. He didn't even have the courtesy to verbally acknowledge receipt of my correspondence so I never got a chance to discuss it with him. I wasn't going to speak first when he'd all but accused me of lying without even hearing what happened to me.

That night I dreamed we were alone in a cathedral. Polished wooden pews shone in the flickering light of tall white candles. He was seated there. I was wearing a long blue satin dress and walked slowly over and sat next to him. This meant I had spiritual truth to impart to this man. When I woke up I had no idea what I was supposed to reveal to him or how to do that at the time.

My son suggested we go to another doctor at the surgery and I agreed with relief. I was confused about why Paul King had reacted that way. He'd come across as professional and caring before. I felt he wanted to talk to me, but he didn't. After that a rape counsellor called me at home. She said the nurse wrote down what I told her, against my wishes. So I didn't have to tell Dr King after all!

The rapist may have left the area but worse was to come. Some bad people moved in next door. They saw I was alone and began to terrorize my family. They were evil, their intent clear. I prayed for the Lord to help me.

A year after that, Alan reintroduced himself to me. We'd initially met at a friend's party. I was soon to learn Alan had a lot of problems. He said he couldn't 'get it up' and asked me to help him. I arranged for him to undergo medical tests to rule out any physical reason. He was not happy to discover his problem was relational.

He was looking for accommodation at the time and I let him stay at my house, hoping he'd protect my family. Allowing him to stay in my home was a big mistake. He was cruel, abusive and used my fear of the tenants next door to intimidate me. He was a worthless witness when it came to the neighbours from hell. The whole time he was there he said he didn't see or hear anything.

He then decided to take a job travelling around the country. I begged him not to leave. I was so thin because of the constant fear I lived in. I'd always loved sleep but my dreams had turned into nightmares. I was afraid to leave the house. I was even afraid in my own home and locked myself in.

Alan would call and hear me weeping. I offered him half my share in the house if he'd come back. He said no. He continued to call and I realized he was getting a kick out of my suffering. The people next door were stalking me and stalking Chris to and from school. They were going through my garbage, throwing broken glass on my lawn, trespassing on my property, blasting out loud music in the middle of the night and round the clock harassment.

I kept reading my Bible day and night, praying to the Lord to get rid of them. I attended local Christian meetings. I rang the police but without a witness they wouldn't listen to me. One officer said he'd protect me if I'd have sex with him; but then he said no, I was too skinny for his tastes. Social workers advised me to leave the area but I couldn't give up the only security my family had.

This went on for three more long years until one day I heard footsteps on the stairs and a booming voice calling my name. I opened the door and there was Russ, the man who claimed he was a woodchopper when he was really a career criminal. I hadn't seen him for years but he was the one person who could stop the creeps next door. He was shocked by my appearance. I was anorexic and literally on my last legs. Russ told them to leave me alone and helped me plant spiky vines to grow along the fence line.

As soon as Alan heard Russ was helping me, he said he was coming back. I tried to help Al for about three years. I had to give love where none was earned to observe his reaction. I analysed all relevant information from his past to give me a map of his life. When he asked to try artificial means of performing sex I agreed, to find out what sort of lover he was. There was no love from him and it was obvious he was thinking corrupt thoughts. No wonder he couldn't get anyone to put up with that. When I tried to tell him he was associating in a way that was not acceptable, he became angry. When I completed my assessment of Alan I tried to tell him the truth but he refused to hear, even becoming violent.

Through all this was the enigma of Paul King. How could I unconditionally love, respect and desire someone I didn't even know? The magnetic attraction was so charged that I almost fell into him if he was near and practically passed out. I wore dark sunnies in the surgery to hide the love shining in my eyes. I could feel his eyes on me like laser beams, illuminating my soul. I tried to envision his embrace but all I could imagine was me fainting of bliss and having a heart attack!

As the ecstasy increased so did my courage to show more of myself to him. I took my sunnies off one day and smiled at him with all the love I was created for. It sounds wild but it seemed like a gale force wind was streaming through my hair as he and I stared at each other. He looked awestruck, scared, and backed up against the wall. We didn't break eye contact until a nurse led me to the examination room. I was slowly coming out of my shell to feel the natural exhilaration of vibrating pure love.

Not long after that his associate I'd been seeing all those years sexually harassed me. After initial shock and fear I experienced the anger of trust betrayed. That quack knew I'd been sexually assaulted which made his behaviour even more despicable. He was a migrant from a culture where women are mistreated.

He then told me to leave the surgery!

I felt he was jealous of his 'friend' and accosted me deliberately. As much as Paul and I tried to hide our feelings, looking back it was obvious there was a major connection between us.

I made a formal complaint about the sexual harassment and from then on I was blacklisted by doctors. I was to learn that making a complaint about one, equated to gross malpractice from all.

I was injured in a fall caused by negligent government workers and went to a clinic where I saw my late husband's last doctor. He'd written a glowing reference about my care of Chris, stating he had 'great respect' for me. I thought *he* wouldn't harm me. He put me on the wrong waiting lists and refused to refer me to appropriate specialists. I was to find out later, after spending months in agony and disability, his referral for me to see specialists at hospital stated his opinion that I was making up the injury for money. No wonder the hospital rated my injury a non-urgent case!

I engaged a lawyer to represent me and the fact that he was also a migrant from the same country as the slimy doctor didn't concern me at the time. I trusted him to do the right thing. He was pathetic, and as the years passed it became obvious. He actually harmed my case. Friends were telling me to hire someone else but that wasn't possible when every doctor I tried to see either refused treatment, or used appointments to write whatever smear they could make up about me, leaving the disabling and life threatening injury undiagnosed and untreated.

Meanwhile, my young son couldn't just run up and hug me as I'd stiffen up and cry out in pain. Household tasks were agonizing and my child had to take over the heavy chores. I rested my back for about two years, hoping and praying for healing.

During this time I heard the old boy was dying of stomach cancer. He'd chosen to put up with disgraceful mistreatment from his wife and it would cost him any hope for peace at the end.

I visited once, bringing flowers and books about positive thinking. When I pulled into their driveway the old girl was out in the yard. Her oily face was twisted with evil as she glared at me with complete hatred. As I exited the vehicle she forced a smile to pretend welcome. I also placed a smile on my face, reminding myself I was there to bring Christian care to a terminally ill relative.

The old girl became angry when I asked her to get a vase for the flowers. The old boy was nice until then. She looked over at him and all of a sudden he was looking for his belt to strap me with! He totally feared her.

I felt so sick I told them I was unwell and got out of there. I wept all the way home. The stories the others told me were true; she was torturing him. I called an elder abuse hotline and was informed that as he wanted to stay with her, there was nothing they could do. The siblings called to tell me about his awful death. They said she was swearing and yelling at him as he lay dying, his diarrhoea spraying the walls and curtains in his death throes.

I became aware my teenage son had been injected, abused and used by a meth gang. My 'little Chris' turned into a lying, thieving, violent criminal constantly running around doing whatever the pushers told him to. He was jailed for bashing an unhappy customer they ripped off. The only living reminder of my husband and great child I was once so proud of, now psychotic and despised by junkies on the street. I again considered suicide.

Determined to move on with my life I tried volunteer work and attended university. Putting more stress and pressure on my spine resulted in extreme pain, increased disability and blood clots. I was refused administration of blood thinning medication. I was also refused a pap smear by multiple doctors despite having two prior operations for pre-cancer cells and being on the Pap Smear Register. Those bastards were not going to stop until I was dead!

On my birthday in 2012, a girlfriend looked up Paul King on the internet as I finally revealed his identity to her. There was the proof he was married as I thought. So why did he have such an overwhelming effect on me? Later that day I googled 'recognizing myself in his eyes' trying to understand why he'd been my reason for living since our eyes first met.

The screen was filled with posts about Twin Flames. As I was reading the various articles the confusion and amazing spiritual attraction finally made sense! I could acknowledge, at least to myself, the connection we shared was divinely inspired. But what could *I* do about it? The guy was married and in a position of authority – as a *doctor* and totally into the things of this world. How could someone like that be *my* Twin? And who was I to be that man's Twin Soul or intrude on his life in any way?

Later that year, I asked a girlfriend to come with me to see if Dr King would assess my injury and perform a pap smear. He hadn't gone out of his way to help me in the past and I didn't think he'd provide medical assistance now. I was brave with Sophie there and dressed to the hilt. She exclaimed at how beautiful she thought I looked. I knew it wasn't the clothes, makeup and hairstyle that made me appear beautiful; it was the anticipation and excitement of seeing my Twin for the first time in years.

As soon as I saw him ecstasy filled my soul. He kept his eyes averted and wouldn't look at me as he entered the surgery. When he finally called me in he told my friend to sit behind him so she couldn't see his face. He had me explain what I needed and then said no he would not render medical aid to me. He actually advised me to go back to the quack that sexually harassed me! I stood to leave and my eyes flashed fire as I asked how he and his cronies could sleep at night. At the door, my voice was full of contempt as I asked if he was going to charge a consultation fee.

Many Twin Flame websites state the Twins are made up of a Spiritual Twin and a Matrix Twin. As the Spiritual Twin I was supposed to be the one to 'wake up' the other. I didn't want to leave this consciousness with any regrets and I knew I'd regret not revealing how much he meant to me.

The bliss engendered by my Twin, re-awakened divine creativity and I wrote a poem for him. It was the only way to express what I'd experienced all these years. I got to say everything I wanted on one page and in a beautiful way. I printed it on embossed paper and savoured the revelation of my soul for weeks, memorizing every line. It was awesome to create the most significant gift to myself and my Twin. Especially the way I included both our names as my name is the feminine of his!

I had to focus on my courage and hand deliver my gift to Paul as it was for his eyes only. I knew he'd be there on the 17th December, 2014 so I entered the surgery. He came to the doorway and I gave it to him. I didn't look at him; just wished him a merry Christmas and left. I felt great relief. I'd overcome my fear and pride to demonstrate unconditional love to someone who behaved as an enemy.

I began writing a journal when I returned home as I was so happy! I'd conquered my greatest fear and told the truth of my heart. Once I did that the synchronicities foretold in Twin Flame posts, blogs and videos began to happen to me. The numbers 11:11, 12:21 etc., began to appear before me. Most mornings a bird would fly onto my balcony and ring golden bells hanging there. I found white feathers all around my garden. Inspiration and information comes to me as I need it and signs and synchronicities keep me moving in the right direction, so I trust that all is well.

A recent dream was an affirmation. I'd gone to see my Twin as I ingested the silver moon and absorbed it willingly. He was seated behind his desk and smiled at me. We laughed together.

I had an important question about our connection and asked him telepathically if I should be visualizing us making love. He appeared as a hologram before me, smiling, and held my hands. This was what I should focus on; both of us equal, face to face, joining spiritually, emotionally, eternally.

The Twin Flame path is one of synchronicity and being guided by my higher self, dreams, signs specific to my union and the experience and knowledge of other Twins. Through the many years I've been on this journey, only the galactic, magnetic attraction of my Twin has opened my heart to the NOW instead of being enshrined in the past.

Twins open each other's heart chakra which in turn activates the higher chakras of both. When they join in the physical they have the power to heal each other completely. The Twin Flame connection is about unconditional love and forgiveness. No matter what he's done, I've loved Paul eternally since our eyes first met.

I'm releasing a lot of patterns and behaviours from the past as they are no longer relevant. I've come full circle back to the little girl who found refuge with the Lord in the branches of a mango tree. I feel my Twin with me and within me and it feels like home. Wow! A deeper awareness and appreciation of our connection just increases with time. He really is my Twin. Through all these years the connection with Paul has been like slowly unwrapping the most beautiful present, layer by layer, until the treasure is fully revealed.

Life as a widow forced me to put up the tough façade I relied on as a child - to protect my family - and the evil actions of others had me considering suicide again. Since meeting my Twin I've held a sacred joy in my heart that makes me want to tear down barriers and live. The connection is resetting and strengthening me to be brave enough to display without fear what I've always been – a blessed child of God.

Whatever the future holds I just trust in the process and treasure every moment of ecstasy that shines from my soul for all to see.

My Twin Soul

Paul

Your Eternal Soul is my Soul's Twin

Through endless ages we yearned to be one again

Recognition of my beauty and power in the mirror of your eyes

Our first glance the most profound moment of my life

A perfect moment when you gently stroked my hand

A fulfilment of ecstasy I am only beginning to understand

Sacred wonder of pristine desire

A passion only Heaven can inspire

Our shared purpose is to exult in completion and perfect peace divine

To worship in the temple of love where there is no memory of time

For you are the magnet and I am the steel

Faint with longing I now have the courage to reveal

I ask nothing yet you give me all

Eternal Love is the Father's Call

In purity and innocence I love completely again

Thank you Lord for the gift of my Twin

Paula

Bradley

They were hungry and sick and ill-treated, too good for this world. Hebrews 11:38

Bradley was the embodiment of Soul Power. He gave freely to others and loved his son. He touched the heart of everyone he met and is remembered with so much love. Though he understood and lived his higher purpose, he *identified* with the world of the ego where he was just some guy trying his best with no one to help him. I also identified with the ego and saw myself as not good enough for him. Both of us were trapped in an illusion of lack through the abuse of others.

At my Twin Flame awakening Bradley appeared in a dream. There was a pristine tropical island with white sand and gently swaying palm trees. The sun shone in a blue sky, the ocean crystal clear. A man arose out of the sea, water glittering like diamonds around his slim hips. I saw it was Bradley. Dolphins were swimming and playing around him. The scene was perfect, with a feeling of complete happiness and peace.

Chris

He does bring about justice at last if you will only wait.
Job 3:12, 14-15

Before we met

Our Wedding Day

Chris hid behind squinted eyes and a tough exterior before he met me. He had the self-respect to know he was created for more than existing in a loveless situation and the courage to follow his heart.

Our wedding photo shows us both glowing with true love. Chris said his time with me was the happiest of his life and I felt exactly the same way about him.

Pure unconditional love with your soul mate is easy and natural when both of you are surrendered to love. To give with all your heart is to know the glory of love.

Paul

This sacred son of God is like yourself; the mirror of his Father's love for you.   ACIM

I was so confused in the years after I met my Twin. I actually thought it could have been a trick from the devil! There was no way I was going to be involved with someone who was not available, and out of touch with his own soul.

Memories of Bradley and my husband had sustained me for years and would do so for the rest of my life. I thought my future was to focus on my dignity as a widow until the time came to unite with my loved ones on the other side. Instead I'm pulled back into the matrix to help my Twin and share my soul contribution for the spiritual awakening of humanity.

In the ego-based matrix my Twin sees himself as a 'big wheel' in the system. The reality is he's part of a ruthless gang, literally above the law. He did nothing about the sexual harassment inflicted on me and tried to force me to go back to the abuser. He refused treatment and was complicit with deception and gross malpractice. *Not* the sort of person I'd ever have anything to do with. His poor "treatment" forced me to stand up for myself.

This is the Twin Flame paradox. Ego driven hypocrites are people I avoid and there's nothing attractive about his behaviour to me. The attraction is that of the soul – my soul. I've grown and matured beyond anything I could have imagined in this life. The Twin Flame experience is about loving and healing me at this stage. I hope Paul is doing the same for himself. He's a man I've never exchanged a personal word with, yet he shares the most intimate spiritual connection with me. The mirror of his soul reflects the beauty of mine perfectly.

The Duty of Love

The Lord has said, 'Leave them; don't touch their filthy things, and I will welcome you and be a Father to you, and you will be My sons and daughters. 2 Corinthians 6:17

Me, Amy & Rita

You may be surrounded by people who persist in sin. This just means they continue to harm others and themselves. They refuse to grow in love and you must protect yourself from them.

Your love and sexual energy are sacred and powerful forces to serve your ascension when applied according to universal law. The responsibility for love is not a chore; it's the key to unlock your power and potential!

Jesus directed His disciples to, 'Love one another as I have loved you.' John 13:34 Open the door to ascension by caring for your own soul and the souls of others. Experience a spiritual high that transcends time and space through the ultimate power of love.

Three Levels of Soul Ascension

His divine power has given us everything needed for life and godliness… Peter 2:3

The greatest power in the universe is already within you! Soul power is your personal connection with God's love. Sharing divine love and choosing to live by universal law aligns us with the power of the Holy Spirit. The Great Spirit brings real comfort and consolation in times of sorrow. In happy times, giving thanks to the Lord for His constant love is as natural as breathing.

Universal energy is always available, so meditate on God's love for you. Listen to your conscience which is the guidance of your higher self, connected through the Holy Spirit to universal wisdom. We have free will over our lives and it's up to us to maintain our part of the connection. Access the power anywhere and anytime you want to. Just open your heart, it really is that easy!

We're here to upgrade to the glory of love and experience spiritual ecstasy. The base level is soul power! Yes, that's right! We are born with a unique eternal soul and through this life we have to learn to value that above all else. Then we must value ourselves to the extent we feel worthy to give and receive love. *It really is all about your own soul.* This basic truth applies to all experiences.

Benefits of soul power include beauty of spirit, the power of love, discernment, courage, kindness, and the humble awareness you are representing the Lord. Evil will not prevail against you. The saints are a perfect example of this. Though many were tortured and murdered for their faith they remained steadfast, astounding their persecutors and strengthening others by their example.

Soul power only increases as you keep on the path that has been made for you. Jesus said, Take my yoke upon you and learn from me, for I am gentle and humble in heart, and you will find rest for your souls. Matthew 11:29 He came into the world for this purpose, to show us the way to Life.

Life *is* love – the only thing worth living and dying for. We are created with the ability to achieve great love through our care for the souls of others.

Centered in sacred respect for your own soul, your primary purpose is to connect with your soul family. With these people you can shine brightly! You are empowered to give and receive pure love knowing the interaction is real and eternal. This engenders peace of heart despite what may be going on around you. These experiences are necessary for the progression and expansion of your soul. Using the power of free will you can decide about any situation and choose to respond with love and courage.

If you feel you've done something wrong, that's just confirmation you're being guided by your conscience and on the right path. Give thanks for the lesson and do what you can to make amends. Mistakes are only learning experiences that facilitate your growth.

Over the course of life our software has been either negative experiences that leave a residue of unhealthy programs, infecting our ability to feel and share love, or positive love experiences through which we attain true spiritual illumination. Apply the lessons you learn to your hard drive – your eternal soul activated by true love. No matter how terrible the past has been, the future can be bright with love and joy!

Transcend the negative ego-based matrix and step up to the magnificence and exultation of spirit that is your birthright. If you think your past is too traumatic to overcome (as I once did) then I pray you are empowered by my journey.

Through ascension we also develop new/ancient abilities such as opening the pineal gland, the transmutation of negative energy, experiencing quantum time and many more. You will awaken to your True Self through the feeling of spiritual ecstasy that transcends all else.

This consciousness is a precious gift where we get to choose how high we ascend. Love and care for yourself. Meditate and spend time in nature to nurture your being. Surrender to the sacred desire to shine with pure love. *You can do it,* and will be motivated, guided and protected by your unique soul power so you can level up to the glory of love and ecstasy of spirit.

Your Sister in Spirit,

Suggested Reading

Bible study is highly recommended. Guidance is specific, especially concerning moral behaviour. Good and evil are real in this world of duality and your Bible has the answers.

You Can Heal Your Life by Louise L Hay is an excellent resource for development of the mental body and when I was ready I attracted this book.

A Course in Miracles published by The Foundation for Inner Peace is for spiritual expansion. So many effective people reference this book. I bought my own copy and within its pages I found illumination and direction for my Twin Flame awakening.

***

These three texts provide valuable assistance for those who choose the path of ascension. Inspired content from evolved people resonates with the eternal and you will intuitively be drawn to those that feel right for your journey. Soul enhancing programs, books, movies and music all contribute to your growth.

Links

https://www.goldenraytwinflameearthangel.com/

Golden Ray Twin Flame Earth Angel Website

https://www.facebook.com/goldenraytwinflameearthangel/?ref=bookmarks

Golden Ray Twin Flame Earth Angel Facebook Page

https://www.facebook.com/paulagoldenraytwinflameearthangel

My Personal Facebook Page

https://www.facebook.com/paulagoldenraytwinflameearthangel/media_set?set=a.1833397603605107&type=3

Unconditional Love and Miracles Facebook Family Album

https://www.facebook.com/paulagoldenraytwinflameearthangel/media_set?set=a.1838605636417637&type=3

My Ego Matrix Twin Flame Facebook Album

https://corruptionandscandalqldhealth.weebly.com/

Corruption and Scandal Qld Health Website – My story

https://www.youtube.com/watch?v=QsX-qOYQCMjI&list=PLgZIUf1y6mMcDoR9T-Txe8GCAi2ecjEkNf

Corruption and Scandal - Medical Malpractice – Australia – My Corruption and Scandal YouTube playlist

https://www.youtube.com/watch?v=qj6Z2crTqlc

Transition to New Earth Mission – My YouTube video

About the Author

Paula is a Twin Flame, Golden Ray spiritual healer, teacher, author, speaker, filmmaker, tarot reader, energetic transmuter and high level empath.

She is an earthangel and new earth community founder for Christ Consciousness, Divine Love, Twin Flames, Universal Self, Transcendental Chakras, The 'Clairs' and Rainbow Rays.

Paula Rule

www.ingramcontent.com/pod-product-compliance
Lightning Source LLC
Chambersburg PA
CBHW062112290426
44110CB00023B/2788